Copyright © Joanna Troughton 1976

First published in 1976, reprinted 1982
Second edition 1986

Blackie and Son Limited
7 Leicester Place, London WC2H 7BP

British Library Cataloguing in Publication Data
Troughton, Joanna
    How the birds changed their feathers.
    I. Title
    823'.914(J)   PZ7

    ISBN 0-216-90084-0

First American edition published in 1986 by
Peter Bedrick Books,
125 East 23rd Street, New York, NY 10010

Library of Congress Cataloging-in-Publication Data
Troughton, Joanna.
    How the birds changed their feathers.

    Summary: A retelling of a South American Indian tale
of how birds, all of which used to be white, came to
have different colors.
    1. Indians of South America—Legends.   2. Birds—
Legends and stories.   (1. Indians of South America—
Legends) I. Title.
F2230.1.F6T76   1986   398.2'4528   86-1251
ISBN 0-87226-080-1

Printed in Great Britain by Cambus Litho, East Kilbride

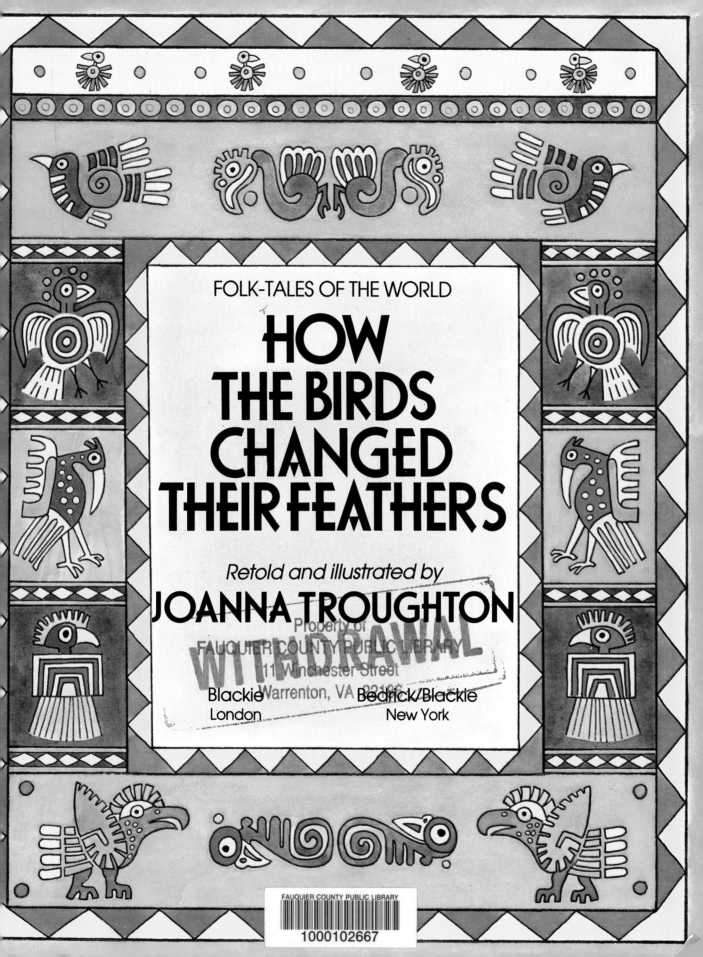

FOLK-TALES OF THE WORLD

HOW THE BIRDS CHANGED THEIR FEATHERS

Retold and illustrated by

JOANNA TROUGHTON

Blackie
London

Bedrick/Blackie
New York

Author's Note

This version of how the birds changed their feathers is told by the Arawak people of Guyana, but it is a myth that occurs in the folklore of many other South American tribes.

In the old days, when men and animals spoke the same language, there lived a boy who loved to hunt birds. In those times, birds were not brightly coloured as they are today, but were white all over. The boy's mother warned him that no good would come of his cruel sport, but he paid her no heed.

Out hunting one day, he found some brightly
coloured stones lying at the river's edge.
They were all the colours of the rainbow.

The boy strung them together on a piece of twine to wear round his neck.

But no sooner had he put the necklace on than a horrible change came over him. . . .

He began to swell.

He swelled and he swelled.

He spread and he spread.

He stretched and he stretched.

Until he wasn't a boy any longer . . .

but a great water snake, with a skin
that was all the colours of the rainbow.

The Rainbow Snake lived deep down in the river, coiled around the trunk of a river tree.

When it was hungry it swam and
slithered to the surface, and waited for
its prey to pass by.
   Every creature lived in fear.

The Chief of the Indians called all the
animals together.

"Whoever kills the Rainbow Snake may
keep the skin as a reward," he declared.

There was much brave talk, but one by
one each animal made an excuse . . .

Then the Cormorant spoke.
  "I'll try," he said.
  "Since I'm a diver, I have the best chance."

Then he took an arrow in his beak . . .

and dived deep into the river.

Down and down he went, until he
saw before him the Rainbow Snake,
lying coiled around the river tree.

Straight at its throat the Cormorant swam.

The Snake awoke with a hiss.

It lifted its great head, twisting and squirming this way and that.

But it was all in vain, for the arrow met its mark, and soon the Snake was dead.

The Indians and the animals
dragged the body ashore.

Then they skinned it.

"I claim the skin as my reward," said the Cormorant.

   The Chief of the Indians laughed to himself. He too wanted the beautiful skin, and he thought he could trick the brave Cormorant out of his prize.

   "Take it," he said, "if you can carry it away!"

   And all the animals began to laugh too.

"That I will," said the Cormorant, and he lifted his head and gave a call.

At first there was silence, but suddenly the air was filled with the beating of wings.

"Birds of the forest," cried the Cormorant.

"Help me to carry away the skin of the Rainbow Snake."

From every direction came the birds.
Twittering and tweeting,
screeching and squawking, down
they swooped.

And taking the skin in their beaks, up they flew again.

The Cormorant flew at the head, and the rainbow skin, like a banner, went streaming away across the sky.

When the birds reached a safe place, the Cormorant
began to share out the skin.

"Let each bird keep the part he has carried," he said.
This the birds did.

And then a strange thing happened. . . .

The birds' feathers began to change.

Birds who carried a red and green piece became red and green themselves.

Birds who carried a blue and yellow piece became blue and yellow.

All the birds changed their feathers,
until they became the colours they
are today.

The Cormorant was not as brightly
coloured as the others, for he had carried
the head which was mainly black.
  But he didn't mind.
  "For an old diver it does very well,"
he said.

The Indians were angry.
From that day to this, they have hunted the birds and have stolen their feathers.